Test 1

- Kompetenzbereiche: Hörverstehen, Wortschatz, Schreiben
- Inhalte: Europäische Städte und Länder; Wortschatz: „Holidays“
- Zeitbedarf: 20 Minuten

Track 1

1 Jenny hält ein Referat über die Länder und Hauptstädte Europas. Tom macht sich Notizen. Ein paar Fakten hat er jedoch durcheinandergebracht. Kreuze jeweils an, ob er etwas richtig *(right)* oder falsch *(wrong)* aufgeschrieben hat. ___ von 6

		right	wrong
a	The Eiffel Tower is not in London.	☐	☐
b	The Tower Bridge is a famous sight in Paris.	☐	☐
c	Madrid is a country in south-western Europe.	☐	☐
d	Hamburg is not a capital.	☐	☐
e	Vienna is the capital of Australia.	☐	☐
f	Rome is a very old city.	☐	☐

2 Trage auf der Karte die englischen Bezeichnungen einiger europäischer Länder ein. ___ von 10

 ✎ 3 Peter, Ann, Liz und Richard erzählen von ihren Sommerferien. Vervollständige die Sätze mithilfe der Wörter auf den Bildern. __ von 23

a I was in ____________ with my ______________.
We went by ______________. We stayed at a _______
______________. We visited many ______________.
My holiday was ____________.

b I was ______________ with _____________________.
We went _______________________________________
__________. The campsite was at the _____________.
We often went ______________________.
My holiday ____________________________________.

c I was with my ____________________ in ____________.
I often played with a ____________ called Susan. She
had a ________________________ and we walked on it.
My holiday was _______________.

d I stayed ____________________ here in ______________.
I played ______________________________. We often
played _____________________. My holiday was
_____________________.

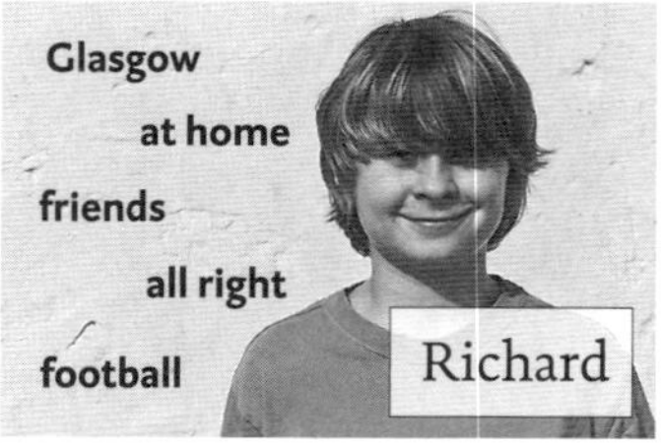

4 Was machst du normalerweise in den Sommerferien? Schreibe fünf Sätze. __ von 10

____

____

____

____

____

____

____

Notenschlüssel

1	2	3	4	5	6
49–45	44–39	38–32	31–25	24–12	11–0

So lange habe ich gebraucht: ____________

So viele Punkte habe ich erreicht: ____________

Klassenarbeit 1

- Kompetenzbereiche: Hörverstehen, Grammatik, Schreiben, Sprachmittlung
- Inhalte: Landeskunde: United Kingdom; Satzstellung, Wiederholung *simple present*
- Zeitbedarf: 30 Minuten

Track 2

1 Höre dir an, was Kimberley über ihre Schule erzählt. Ergänze die folgenden Sätze jeweils mit dem richtigen Wort aus dem Kasten. ___ von 11

class – Edinburgh – favourite – goes – guitar – language – likes – lunch – name – old people – wear

a Kimberley's family ________________ is Reed.

b She ____________ to school in ________________.

c She is in ____________ 4S.

d The pupils ______________ school uniforms at Drummond Community High School (DCHS).

e Kimberley has ______________ at school.

f Her ________________ subject is P.E.

g She ______________ to play the ______________.

h DCHS organized a lot of activities for ________________ in a home.

i Kimberley goes to a ________________ club.

2 Höre dir noch einmal an, was Kimberley erzählt. Antworte dann mit Kurzantworten: *"Yes, …"* oder *"No, …"* ___ von 4

a Does Kimberley go to school by bike? No, she doesn't.

b Does she like sport lessons? ______________

c Does she learn French at school? ______________

d Do the pupils wear jeans at school? ______________

e Do the pupils have lunch at school? ______________

3 *School in Scotland.* Bilde Sätze, indem du die Wörter in die richtige Reihenfolge bringst. ___ von 6

a School ____
at 9 o'clock – starts – in Scotland – ~~school~~

b ____
must – pupils – school uniforms – wear

c ____
have – at school – the pupils – lunch

d ____

they – every – tests – week – have

e ____

in the afternoon – at half past three – lessons – finish

f ____

the pupils – their homework – do – school – after

4 Vivien, Allan, Gary und Ella leben in Großbritannien. Sieh dir die Landkarte an und vervollständige die Sätze. ___ von 6

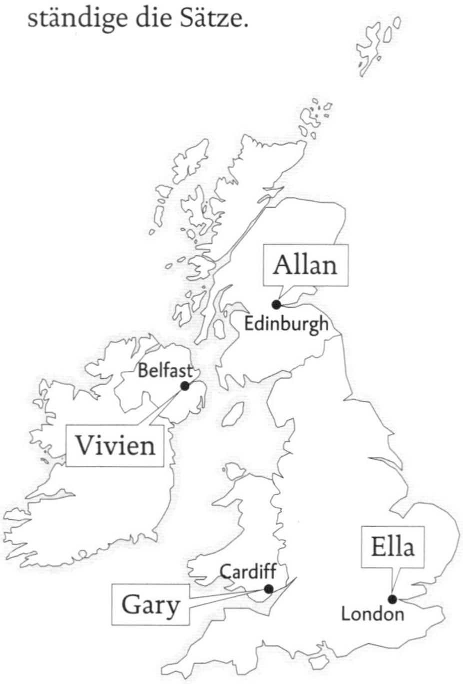

a *Ella is from England. She lives in London.*

b Allan ____

____

c ____.

____ Northern Ireland.

d ____.

____ from Wales.

5 Sieh dir die Bilder an. Schreibe dann die passende Frage oder die passende Antwort auf. ___ von 8

a Does Gary go to school by bike?

No, he doesn't. He ...

b ____

Yes, they do.

c ____

Yes, she does.

d Do the Browns have a cat?

____

6 Fiona und Ryan unterhalten sich. Schreibe auf Englisch auf, was sie sagen.

5

___ von 17

Fiona …

… fragt, ob er oft fernsieht.

____

____

Ryan …

… sagt, dass er immer am Samstag fernsieht.

____

____

… fragt, was seine Lieblingssendung *(show)* ist.

____

____

… sagt, dass er gern *Sport live* ansieht.

____

____

… fragt, wann die Sendung kommt.

____

____

… sagt, um 5 Uhr nachmittags.

____

____

… fragt, ob sie auch gerne Krimis *(thrillers)* sieht.

____

____

… verneint.

____

… sagt, dass sie gerne Quizshows sieht.

____

____

Notenschlüssel

1	2	3	4	5	6
52–47	46–39	38–31	30–23	22–11	10–0

So lange habe ich gebraucht: ______________

So viele Punkte habe ich erreicht: ______________

Test 2

- Kompetenzbereiche: Hörverstehen, Leseverstehen, Wortschatz
- Inhalte: Wortschatz: „Elektronische Geräte“
- Zeitbedarf: 10 Minuten

Track 3

1 Olivia erzählt von einer Party, auf der sie eingeladen war.
Höre dir den Text zuerst an und ergänze dann die fehlenden Wörter. ___ von 1

Last ____________________ I was at a party.

Isabella, my best friend, ____________________ also invited.

The party ______________ in Alisa's house, but in a shed in their garden. Alisa is a school friend of mine.

The party was from 6 o'clock till 9 o'clock in the ____________________.

There __________________ lots of children, we __________________ only five.

It was quite __________________ in the shed.

There was no electric ____________________.

But there were some candles on the ____________________.

The music was ________________ loud and really cool.

We all liked the songs.

Only Johnny, their ________________, wasn't very happy. He hates loud music.

2 Schreibe jeweils das englische Wort für die folgenden Gegenstände auf. ___ von 5

___ von 6

3 Lies dir den folgenden Text durch.
Bringe die Bilder danach in die richtige Reihenfolge (1–6).

One evening Rod said to his brother Kevin: "Let's play football in the street in front of our house." So they went out and kicked the ball to each other. Suddenly Rod kicked the ball over the fence and it landed in the neighbour's garden. Rod rang the bell. Mr Shannon came to the window on the first floor and said: "Wait a minute. I'll give you the ball back." But Mr Shannon wasn't fast enough. When the Shannons' dog Buddy saw the ball, he wanted to play with it. He pushed it and bit into it. The ball was ruined before Mr Shannon could give it back to the boys. Mr Shannon said he was sorry for that, but he couldn't do anything about it. The boys went home sadly with the ruined football.

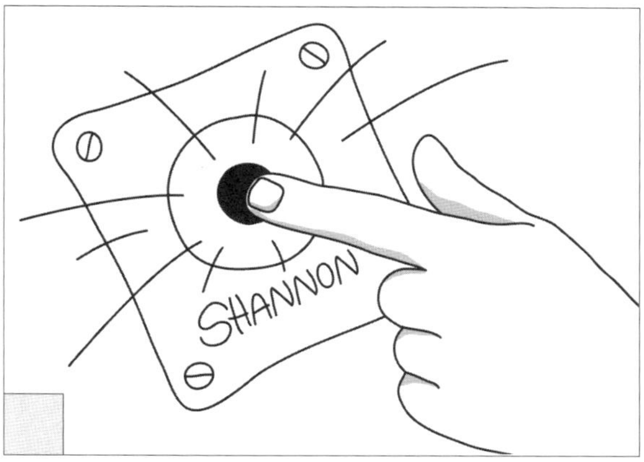

Notenschlüssel

1	2	3	4	5	6
22–20	19–17	16–14	13–11	10–5	4–0

So lange habe ich gebraucht: ____________

So viele Punkte habe ich erreicht: ____________

Klassenarbeit 2

- Kompetenzbereiche: Leseverstehen, Wortschatz, Grammatik, Sprachmittlung
- Inhalte: Ordinal- und Kardinalzahlen, *must/mustn't, can/can't*, Formen von *to be* im *simple past*
- Zeitbedarf: 30 Minuten

1 Schreibe das Geburtsjahr folgender berühmter Leute in Ziffernform auf. ___ von 4

William Shakespeare

The most famous English writer was born in

___

fifteen sixty-four

Isaac Newton

The great English scientist was born in

___

sixteen fourty-three

Lady Gaga

The famous American singer was born in

___

nineteen eighty-six

J. K. Rowling

The author of the Harry Potter books was born in

___

nineteen sixty-five

2 Lies den Text und bearbeite dann die dazugehörige Aufgabe. ___ von 13

Cities in the United Kingdom

London is the capital of the United Kingdom and its biggest city. It has lots of inhabitants *(Einwohner)*, almost eight million people. In Europe only Moscow in Russia is bigger. But there are other interesting towns in England, Wales, Scotland and Northern Ireland.
Brighton, in the south of England, has about one hundred fifty-five thousand inhabitants. An old town in the north of England is **York**. It's quite small, but it's a beautiful town. It has about one hundred thirty-five thousand inhabitants.
Now let's have a look at Scottish cities. The capital of Scotland is **Edinburgh**, with about four hundred eighty-six thousand inhabitants. But the biggest city in Scotland is **Glasgow** with about five hundred ninety-two thousand inhabitants.
The capital of Wales is **Cardiff**. About three hundred forty-one thousand people live there. That is not much compared to London. But it is bigger than **Belfast**, the capital of Northern Ireland, with approximately two hundred sixty-five thousand people.

Bringe die Städte der Größe nach in die richtige Reihenfolge. Die Einwohnerzahlen sind bereits in Ziffern angegeben. Schreibe die Ordnungszahlen (1st, 2nd, etc.) aus.

		city	inhabitants
1st			8 000 000
2nd			592 000
3rd			486 000
4th			341 000
5th			265 000
6th			155 000
7th	seventh		135 000

3 Du sagst auf Englisch, dass …

___ von 9

… du letzte Woche mit einer Freundin im Kino warst.

… der Film nicht gut war.

… der Titel *(title)* des Films „Batman Returns" war.

… dein Bruder im Fußballstadion war.

… das Spiel ziemlich langweilig war.

4 Was bedeuten die Zeichen? Ergänze die Sätze mit *must*, *mustn't*, *can* oder *can't*. Manchmal musst du auch noch ein weiteres Wort einfügen, sodass der Satz einen Sinn ergibt. ___ von 8

a You ____________ take photos here.

b Cyclists ____________ ride their bikes here.

c Drivers ____________ turn right.

d Drivers ____________ ____________ here.

e Drivers ____________ ____________ here.

f Drivers ____________ drive faster than 30 km/h.

Notenschlüssel

1	2	3	4	5	6
30–28	27–23	22–18	17–13	12–6	5–0

So lange habe ich gebraucht: ____________

So viele Punkte habe ich erreicht: ____________

Test 3

- Kompetenzbereiche: Hörverstehen, Wortschatz, Grammatik
- Inhalte: Wortschatz: Gefühlsausdrücke; Grammatik: unregelmäßige Verben, Satzstellung
- Zeitbedarf: 15 Minuten

Track 4

1 *At the electronics shop:* Höre dir das Gespräch zwischen dem Verkäufer und der Kundin an. Entscheide dann, ob die Aussagen richtig *(right)* oder falsch *(wrong)* sind. ___ von 7

		right	wrong
a	Die Kundin betritt das Geschäft am Vormittag.	☐	☐
b	Die Kundin möchte ein Smartphone ohne Kamera kaufen.	☐	☐
c	Der Verkäufer sagt, dass das blaue Smartphone 199,99 £ kostet.	☐	☐
d	Der Kundin sind auch 79,99 £ zu teuer für ein Smartphone.	☐	☐
e	Die Kundin möchte ein Smartphone in rosa.	☐	☐
f	Das Smartphone für 79,99 £ gibt es auch in rosa.	☐	☐
g	Die Kundin geht ohne Smartphone.	☐	☐

2 Ordne die Adjektive den jeweiligen Bildern zu: tired – crazy – angry – happy – sad – grumpy ___ von 6

3 Unregelmäßige Verben: Ergänze die Tabelle mit den richtigen englischen Verbformen. ___ von 14

simple present	simple past	Grundform (deutsch)
1 we find	we found	*finden*
2 I m___	I ___	*treffen*
3 they ___	they ___	*denken*
4 he h___	he ___	*haben*
5 you t___	you ___	*nehmen*
6 she t___	she ___	*erzählen, sagen*
7 he ___	he w___	*sein*
8 she w___	she ___	*schreiben*

12 4 *Peggy's birthday:* Bringe die einzelnen Satzteile in die richtige Reihenfolge. ___ von 7

a I had – last Friday – a birthday party

b wore – dress – I – my red and white

c some – did – my father – magic tricks

d very exciting – was – that

e from my family – a lot of – I got – presents

f a birthday cake – my older sister – for me – with candles – made

g were – the grilled – sausages – very good

Notenschlüssel

1	2	3	4	5	6
34–31	30–27	26–22	21–15	14–10	9–0

So lange habe ich gebraucht: ___

So viele Punkte habe ich erreicht: ___

Klassenarbeit 3

- Kompetenzbereiche: Hörverstehen, Leseverstehen, Grammatik
- Inhalte: *simple past*, Modalverben (*must/mustn't, should, could*), *some/any, something/anything*
- Zeitbedarf: 30 Minuten

Track 5

1 Charlie kommt aus der Schule nach Hause. Höre dir an, was er seiner Mutter über die ersten Eisenbahnen erzählt. Unterstreiche dann die richtigen Satzteile. ___ von 7

a The first steam locomotive was built in *England / Germany/ Ireland.*

b The most famous early locomotive in England was called *"Racket" / "Rocket" / "Adler".*

c It won a locomotive competition *in Liverpool / in Rainhill / in Manchester.*

d Its top speed was *48 km/h / 84 km/h / 65 km/h.*

e The first locomotive in Germany ran in *1835/ 1853 / 1830.*

f The driver of the Adler was *William Wilson / Joseph Locke / Robert Stephenson.*

g The Adler was built in *England / Germany / Nuremberg.*

2 Lies den folgenden Text über eine kleine Katze. Beantworte dann die Fragen zum Text (Kurzantworten). ___ von 7

Koshka's accident

It happened last Saturday afternoon. The Shorts were at the supermarket. When they came home to their flat on the first floor, Martin called for the cat: "Koshka, where are you? Come here, I've got something for you." Koshka was a young cat, only three months old. Martin called again, but Koshka didn't come. Mrs Short looked at the balcony door; it was open. The whole family went onto the balcony. They heard a soft voice from the playground. They looked down and saw Koshka sitting in the sandpit *(Sandkasten)* crying. Martin quickly ran down the stairs. He carefully picked Koshka up and carried her upstairs. Mr Short took her to the vet at once. She had a broken leg and had to stay at the vet's for two days. Then Martin and his father took her home. After two weeks she could walk again. Since that day *(seitdem)* the Shorts always close the door to the balcony when they go away.

a What animal do the Shorts have? *a cat*

b Where were the Shorts on that Saturday afternoon? ______

c On which floor is the Shorts' flat? ______

d Who saw the open balcony door first? ______

e Was Koshka on the balcony? ______

f Where was Koshka when they saw her? ______

g What had she hurt? ______

h What do the Shorts do now whenever they go away? ______

3 Eine Nachbarin der Shorts erzählt Mrs Short, was sie gestern gesehen hat. Ergänze die Sätze mit den richtigen *simple past*-Formen. ___ von 9

"I ______________ (look) out of the window. I ______________ (see) the door of the balcony open and Koshka ______________ (come) out. First she ______________ (play) with a peg *(Wäscheklammer)*. Then she ______________ (jump) on the railing *(Geländer)* of the balcony. First she ______________ (go) along the railing. Then she ______________ (is) at the corner of the balcony railing. She ______________ (watch) the birds at the playground. I ______________ (call): "Koshka, go down the railing!", but she didn't listen. Then I had to go and take my grandson Bob to his music lesson."

4 Letzten Donnerstag war Billy krank. Was hat er gemacht bzw. nicht gemacht?
Sieh dir die Stichwörter in den Klammern an und bilde ganze Sätze im *simple past*. ___ von 6

a *He stayed in bed.* (stay in bed)
b *He didn't go to school.* (not go to school)
c ______________ (phone a friend)
d ______________ (not visit his grandma)
e ______________ (watch TV)
f ______________ (have some biscuits)
g ______________ (drink a lot of tea)
h ______________ (not speak very much)

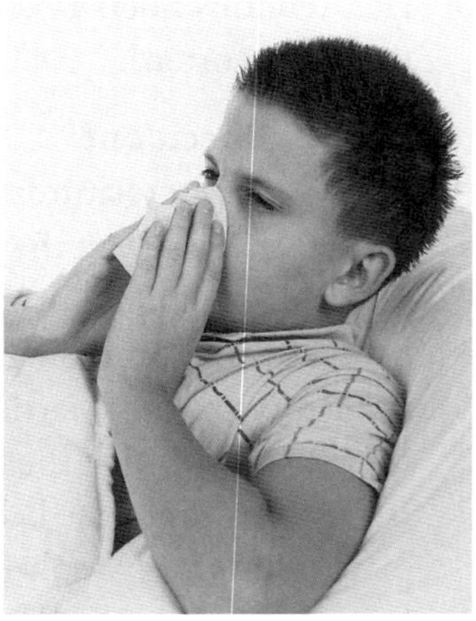

5 *What must Christopher do? What mustn't he do?* Was muss Christopher tun und was darf er nicht tun? Sieh dir die Beispiele an und schreibe die restlichen Sätze auf. ___ von 5

His mum says to Christopher:

a "Christopher, don't watch TV before you've done your homework."
He mustn't watch TV. He must do his homework first.

b "Clean your shoes. They are very dirty."
He must clean his shoes because they are very dirty.

c "Take the dog for a walk."
____

d "Don't go to visit your friend now. Clean your room first."

___

e "Don't play computer games all day."

___

f "Open the bathroom window."

___

6 Füge die Wörter im Kasten an der richtigen Stelle in die Lücken ein. ___ von 6

shouldn't – could – some – any – something – anything

a Timmy, you ___ eat too many sweets!

b Timmy: I didn't eat ___ sweets last week.

c ___ you open the window, please? It's so hot in here!

d Waiter: "Would you like ___ else?"

e Guest: "I would like ___ to drink."

f Waiter: "I could offer you ___ delicious red wine."

Notenschlüssel

1	2	3	4	5	6
40–37	36–32	31–26	25–20	19–9	8–0

So lange habe ich gebraucht: ___

So viele Punkte habe ich erreicht: ___

Test 4

- Kompetenzbereiche: Hörverstehen, Wortschatz, Grammatik
- Inhalte: Wegbeschreibung; Wortschatz: Präpositionen; Grammatik: *present progressive*, *of*-Genitiv
- Zeitbedarf: 15 Minuten

Track 6

1 Vier Personen fragen nach dem Weg. Höre dir die Dialoge an. Beschrifte dann die einzelnen Gebäude auf dem Stadtplan jeweils mit *toilet*, *post office*, *hospital* oder *tourist office*. Höre dir die Dialoge noch einmal an und markiere die Wege, die beschrieben werden. Die Wegbeschreibung beginnt immer an der markierten Stelle. ___ von 8

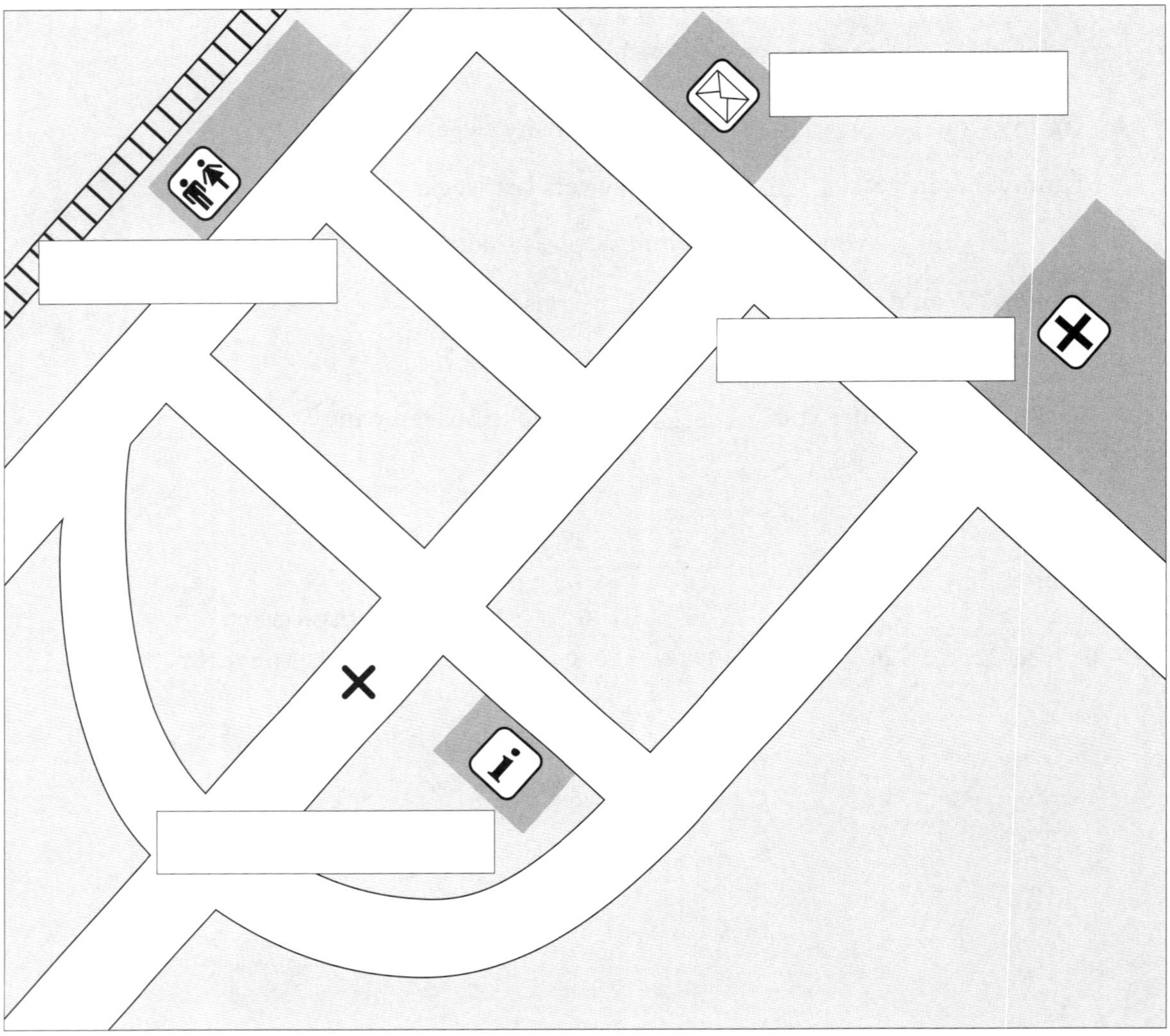

2 Übersetze zuerst die englischen Wörter im Kasten. Welche der ins Englische übersetzten Wörter reimt sich mit den englischen Wörtern unten? ___ von 7

Tasche – Buch – bringen – denken – lesen – ~~Suppe~~ – hell – Park

group	dark	flag	fight	drink	feed	look	thing
soup	______	______	______	______	______	______	______

3 *Brian is talking about his favourite sport.*
Setze die richtigen Präpositionen aus dem Kasten ein. ___ von 7

at – with – about – in – on – from – for

My birthday will be ______ Friday.

Maybe I'll get some table tennis balls ______ my parents. I'm very good ________ table tennis. My friend Dominic often plays _________ me. I asked him: "What ________ a game of table tennis?" I'm waiting ______ him now. I've already put up the table ______ the garden.

4 Schreibe die passenden Antworten zu den Fragen auf. ___ von 8

a What are you reading? I'm ______________________________ a book.

b Who are you talking to? ______________________________ to Mary.

c What are Lisa and Tom drinking? ______________________________ some tomato juice.

d Why are you two laughing? ______________________________ because the picture is so funny.

e Where is Ben playing football? ______________________________ on the playground.

5 Was hat Mrs Warren gekauft? Sieh dir die Bilder an und vervollständige die Lücken. ___ von 6

Mrs Warren bought ...

- three ______________________________,
- a ____________________ chocolates,
- ______________________________ jelly beans,
- a packet ______________________________,
- ______________________________ milk.

Notenschlüssel

1	2	3	4	5	6
36–33	32–28	27–23	22–18	17–8	7–0

So lange habe ich gebraucht: ____________

So viele Punkte habe ich erreicht: ____________

Klassenarbeit 4

- Kompetenzbereiche: Leseverstehen, Grammatik, Sprachmittlung
- Inhalte: *present progressive,* Fragen bilden mit Fragewörtern, *some/any*
- Zeitbedarf: 30 Minuten

1 Lies dir den folgenden Text durch und bearbeite dann die Aufgabe. ___ von 8

The hamster at school

Ella and Lily are friends. They are in the same class, too. One day, it was 31st March, Ella wasn't at school because she had a terrible cold. So Ella phoned Lily to ask her about the homework. Lily said, "We're lucky, Ella, there is no homework for tomorrow. But, wait a minute, Mrs Silverstone told us to bring our pets to school tomorrow. I'll bring my dog. Can you bring your hamster?" "Sure I can do that," answered Ella.

The next morning Ella put her hamster in a cage. Her mother took her with the hamster to school in the car. Ella went into the classroom and put the cage on her table. When she was at her table and looked around, she saw that nobody else had a pet with them. At that moment Mrs Silverstone, the teacher, came into the classroom. She looked at the cage with Ella's hamster and asked: "Ella, why did you bring a hamster to school?" Now all the other children laughed and shouted, "April fools day! April fools day!" Mrs Silverstone smiled: "Oh, I see, Ella, today is 1st April. They played a trick on you, but never mind. Then we'll have a lesson about hamsters today, and your hamster will be very useful to us."

Füge die folgenden Satzteile zusammen:

1	Ella and Lily are	a	Ella and Lily's teacher.
2	Ella wasn't	b	a pet with them.
3	She was	c	in the same class.
4	Ella brought	d	the hamster for a lesson.
5	Ella put	e	her hamster to school.
6	Mrs Silverstone is	f	an April fool's trick on Ella.
7	Nobody else had	g	at school on the last day of March.
8	The pupils had played	h	ill.
9	Mrs Silverstone used	i	the cage with the hamster on her table.

1	2	3	4	5	6	7	8	9
c								

2 Hier siehst du ein Urlaubsbild der Familie Smith. Mr Smith erzählt, was auf dem Foto gerade geschieht. Vervollständige die Sätze.

___ von 6

a Here we are ______________________ *(sit)* in front of our tent. It's a wonderful morning.

b The sun ______________________ *(shine)*.

c We ______________________ *(have)* breakfast.

d Kristy, my wife, ______________________ *(wear)* a big hat and sunglasses.

e Our children ______________________ *(play)* cards.

f Timmy, our dog, ______________________ *(watch)* them.

20 3 *A fine summer's day:* Schreibe zu den Antworten die passenden Fragen auf.
Verwende dabei folgende Fragewörter jeweils einmal: *what – when – where – why – who* ___ von 5

Example: What is Vincent drinking?
Vincent is drinking a glass of orange juice.

a ______________________________

Vincent is eating a piece of cake.

b ______________________________

He is sitting in the garden.

c ______________________________

He is sitting in the garden because it is a warm and sunny day.

d ______________________________

His dog Timmy is lying next to him.

e ______________________________

At around 12 o'clock Vincent is having some lunch.

4 Dies ist der Kühlschrank der Familie Smith. Welche Lebensmittel kannst du dort finden? Vervollständige die Sätze. Verwende *some* oder *any.* ___ von 9

a There is ______________ jam in the fridge.

b There is also ______________ cheese in it.

c But there aren't ______________ sausages in it.

d There ______________ apples.

e Is there ______________ salad in the fridge? – ______________.

f And there are ______________ eggs in it.

g There is also ______________

____

____

(name two more things)

5 Patrick ist in London und möchte ein Souvenir für seinen Vater kaufen. Schreibe den Dialog auf Englisch.

___ von 12

Patrick …

Shop assistant …

Patrick … sagt, dass er ein Geschenk für seinen Vater kaufen möchte.

Shop assistant … fragt, was er kaufen möchte.

Patrick … sagt, er weiß es nicht.

Shop assistant … fragt, ob sein Vater Bier mag.

Patrick … bejaht.

Shop assistant … fragt, ob ihm das Bierglas mit dem Big Ben darauf gefällt.

Patrick … sagt, dass es schön ist.

… fragt nach dem Preis.

Shop assistant … sagt, dass es nicht teuer ist und nur 3,50 £ kostet.

Patrick … sagt, dass er es nimmt.

… bittet die Verkäuferin, es in eine Schachtel zu tun.

Notenschlüssel

1	2	3	4	5	6
40–37	36–32	31–26	25–20	19–9	8–0

So lange habe ich gebraucht: ____________

So viele Punkte habe ich erreicht: ____________

Test 5

- Kompetenzbereiche: Hörverstehen, Grammatik, Wortschatz
- Inhalte: Grammatik: Steigerung der Adjektive / Vergleiche; Wortschatz: *opposites*
- Zeitbedarf: 15 Minuten

Track 7

1 Die Familien Todd, Hoon, Macmillan und Hillstone erzählen davon, was sie in ihren Ferien unternommen haben. ___ von 4

a Höre dir die Texte an und schreibe die Namen der Familien unter die richtigen Bilder. Zwei Bilder passen nicht.

____

____

____

____

____

____

b Höre dir die Texte noch einmal an und entscheide, ob die Aussagen richtig oder falsch sind. ___ von 9

	right	wrong
• The weather was nice when the Hoons went along Hadrian's Wall.	☐	☐
• Hadrian's Wall was built by the Romans.	☐	☐
• Mr Todd is a football player.	☐	☐
• Old Trafford is the stadium of Manchester City.	☐	☐
• Manchester United's stadium is much bigger than Manchester City's stadium.	☐	☐
• The Macmillans stayed in a big city in the Lake District.	☐	☐
• The Macmillans visited a pencil museum.	☐	☐
• The Hillstones went to York for the first time.	☐	☐
• The Hillstones took part in a tour around the city of York.	☐	☐

2 *The highest mountains in Europe.* ___ von 4

Vervollständige den Text mit der jeweils passenden Steigerungsform von *high*.

Monte Rosa is a very high mountain in the Alps.

It is __the highest__ mountain in Switzerland.

Mont Blanc is ____________ mountain in France.

Mont Blanc is ____________ ______ Monte Rosa.

At 4 810 m it is ____________ mountain in Europe.

3 Vergleiche die folgenden Fischarten miteinander. ___ von 11

One of the *(expensive)* ______ ____________ fish is the Koi. You must keep koi in a little pond. An aquarium is too small for them. Some people think they are *(nice)* ____________ fish in the world. Other people think betta are even *(nice)* ____________ ______ the Koi. But you must keep them alone in an aquarium because they are very aggressive. Guppies are *(easy)* ____________ to keep and quite popular. But goldfish are *(popular)* ____________ ____________ ______ the guppies. They are one of the *(popular)* ____________ ____________ aquarium fish in the world.

4 Finde das jeweilige Gegenteil der folgenden Adjektive. ___ von 10

a exciting / __boring__

b young / ____________

c expensive / ____________

d ugly / ____________

e early / ____________

f difficult / ____________

g sad / ____________

h bad / ____________

i short / ____________

j slow / ____________

k small / ____________

Notenschlüssel

1	2	3	4	5	6
38–34	33–29	28–24	23–19	18–9	8–0

So lange habe ich gebraucht: ____________

So viele Punkte habe ich erreicht: ____________

Klassenarbeit 5

- Kompetenzbereiche: Leseverstehen, Grammatik
- Inhalte: Steigerungsformen der Adjektive; *could/couldn't (simple past)*; Frage und Verneinung im *simple past*
- Zeitbedarf: 30 Minuten

1 Lies dir den folgenden Text durch und bearbeite dann die Aufgaben. ___ von 12

The ducks and the salad

The Masons had a small garden behind their house. Their neighbours, the Ratcliffs, were farmers and they had ducks. In May Mrs Mason always planted some vegetables. She looked after the plants and watered them every day.

After two months the vegetables looked ripe, and Mrs Mason thought: "Tomorrow we're going to have our first salad." But the next morning, Ricky, the Masons' little son, ran into the house. He shouted: "Mum, Mum, the Ratcliffs' ducks are in our garden and they are eating our salad!" Mrs Mason hurried out, but it was too late. The garden was ruined. The ducks had eaten most of the plants.

Mrs Ratcliff felt very sorry for Mrs Mason, but she couldn't do anything about it. Some months later, however, a few days before Christmas, Mrs Ratcliff took a parcel to Mrs Mason. When Mrs Mason opened it, she found a nice fat duck and a piece of paper that said: "Enjoy your salad."

Beantworte zunächst die folgende Frage auf Deutsch:

a Weshalb hat Mrs Ratcliff der Familie Mason eine Ente geschenkt?

____

____

Vervollständige dann die folgenden Sätze auf Englisch.

b The Masons had ____________________ behind their house.

c Their neighbours, the Ratcliffs, were ____________________.

d Every year in May Mrs Mason ____________________.

e One morning Ricky shouted: "The Ratcliffs' ducks ____________________

____________________.

f Mrs Ratcliff ran out but ____________________.

g The garden ____________________.

h The ducks had eaten ____________________.

i Mrs Ratcliff felt ____________________.

j Some days before Christmas ____________________

____________________.

k In the parcel there was ____________ and

____________________.

2 *Comparing.*
Vervollständige die folgende Tabelle mit den richtigen Steigerungsformen der Adjektive.

___ von 7

cheap		*the cheapest*
popular	*more popular*	
early	*earlier*	
good		
bad		

3 Sieh dir das Bild der Familie an und bearbeite die folgenden Aufgaben.

___ von 16

a Schreibe die richtigen Steigerungsformen der Adjektive in die Lücken.

This is my father. He is 42 years old. He is (old) ____________________ in our family. I've got two sisters, Leah and Victoria. This is Leah; she is my (young) ____________________ sister. She is (small) ____________________ in our family. Victoria plays the piano and the violin. She is (musical) ____________________ member of our family. Can you see my brother Andrew? It is not difficult because he is (tall) ____________________. Can you find me? I always buy (beautiful) ____________________ and (modern) ____________________ clothes I can find in the shops. And there is our mother. I think she is (busy) ______________, (nice) ____________________ and (intelligent) ____________________ woman in the world. We all love her.

b Schreibe auf Englisch die Familienmitglieder neben die Ziffern.

1 ____________________ 2 ____________________ 3 ____________________

4 ____________________ 5 ____________________ 6 ____________________

4 Allan und sein Vater haben Madame Tussauds besucht. Was konnten sie dort tun und was nicht? Vervollständige die Sätze und verwende dabei folgende Verben: ___ von 5

touch – take (2×) – smoke – buy

a Allan's father ______________________ cigarettes.

b Allan ______________________ photos of the wax models.

c They ______________________ their dog with them.

d They ______________________ some souvenirs.

e They ______________________ the wax models.

5 Bernard war in London. Sein Freund Peter stellt ihm einige Fragen. Was hat er gefragt und was hat Bernard geantwortet? Gib Kurzantworten. ___ von 10

a *Did you like London?*
Yes, I really liked it there.

b How long ________ you __________ in London? I stayed in London for five days.

c ______________________ with your family? – Yes, I did. I went with my parents and my brother.

d ______________________ at a hotel? – No, we didn't. We stayed at a friend's house.

e Was it your first time in London? – No, it ______________________.

f ______________________
No, we didn't see the Queen.

g Did you see "The Shard", the highest building in London? – Yes, we ______________________.

h Did you go on a boat tour on the River Thames? – No, we ______________________.

i __________ your parents and your brother like London, too?
Yes, ______________________.

6 Die Fishers unterhalten sich über ihre Ferien.
Schreibe auf Englisch auf, was sie sagen.

___ von 14

a Mrs Fisher findet, dass ihre letzte Reise nach Irland sehr schön war.

b Sie möchte im nächsten Jahr wieder nach Irland fahren.

c Kristin sagt, dass sie mit ihren Eltern mit in Urlaub fährt, wenn *(if)* sie nicht nach Irland fahren.

d Rod sagt, dass er dieses Jahr nicht wegfahren will.

e Mrs Fisher fragt ihn, was er (dann) tun wird.

f Er sagt, dass er zu Hause bleiben wird. Er wolle sein Geld für ein neues Fahrrad sparen *(save)*.

g Mrs Fisher meint, dass sie darüber sprechen können.

Notenschlüssel

1	2	3	4	5	6
64–57	56–48	47–39	38–30	29–14	13–0

So lange habe ich gebraucht: ___

So viele Punkte habe ich erreicht: ___

Test 6

- Kompetenzbereiche: Hörverstehen, Wortschatz
- Inhalte: Grammatik: *will-future*; Wortschatz: „Wetter“, allgemeiner Wortschatz
- Zeitbedarf: 15 Minuten

Track 8

1 Höre dir das Gespräch zwischen Mrs Moore und Mr Cain zweimal an. Unterstreiche dann die richtigen Satzteile. ___ von 9

a Is Mrs Moore talking to Mr Cain in the morning or in the evening?

b Have they had fine weather or bad weather for a long time?

c Are they talking to each other in June or July?

d Are the Moores going to Spain or to Italy?

e Are the Cains going on holiday at exactly the same time as the Moores or one day later?

f Are the Moores going to Spain by car or by plane?

g Are the Moores going on holiday because they don't like the weather at home or because they want to visit their son?

h Do the Moores have a dog or a cat?

i Is the Smiths' son coming from Australia or from Austria?

j Will the Moores be away for two weeks or for three weeks?

2 *The weather in Europe.* Sieh dir die Tabelle über das Wetter in Europa an und beantworte dann die Fragen auf der nächsten Seite in ganzen Sätzen. Schreibe auch auf, wie das Wetter sein wird, wenn du die Frage verneinst. ___ von 7

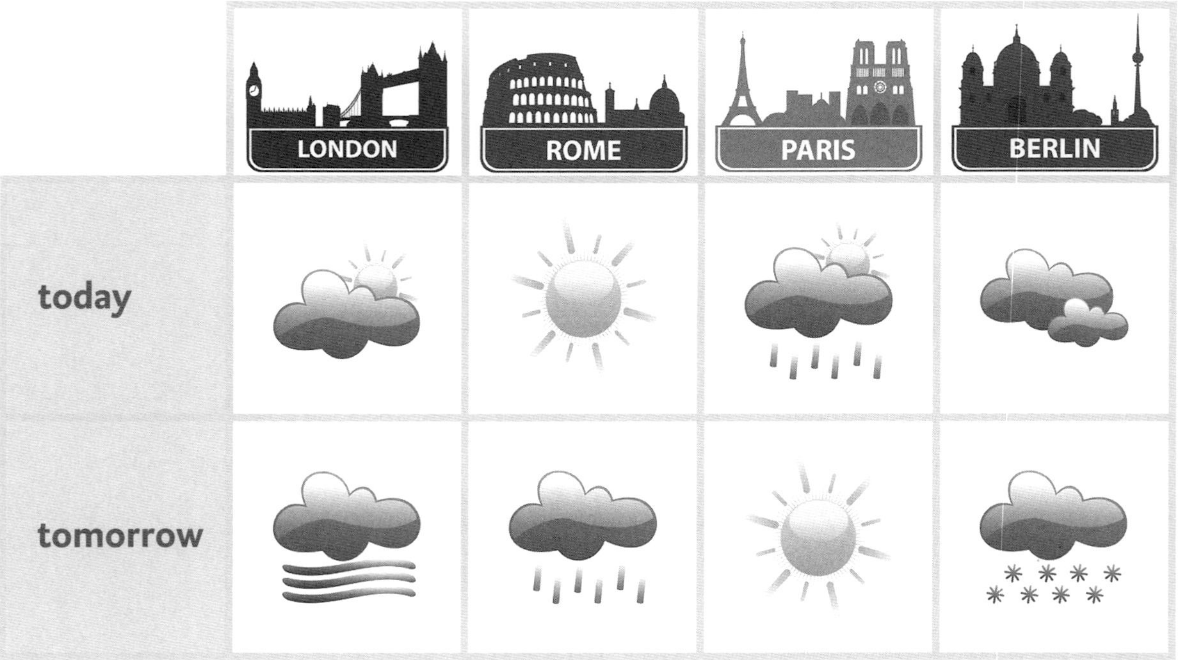

a What's the weather like in Rome today?

____

b What will the weather be like in Rome tomorrow?

____

c Will it rain in London tomorrow?

____

d Is it sunny in Berlin today?

____

e Will it snow in Berlin tomorrow?

____

f Write two sentences about the weather in Paris today and tomorrow.

____

____

3 *Odd one out.* Streiche das Wort durch, das jeweils nicht in die Reihe passt. ___ von 5

a morning – evening – clock – afternoon – night

b year – autumn – spring – winter – summer

c carrot – chocolate – bread – cheeseburger – cook

d longer – better – driver – higher – nicer

e cloudy – sunny – snowy – busy – rainy

Notenschlüssel

1	2	3	4	5	6
21–19	18–16	15–13	12–10	9–5	4–0

So lange habe ich gebraucht: __________

So viele Punkte habe ich erreicht: __________

Klassenarbeit 6

- Kompetenzbereiche: Hörverstehen, Leseverstehen, Grammatik, Schreiben
- Inhalte: Grammatik: *will-future*, über die Zukunft schreiben
- Zeitbedarf: 30 Minuten

Track 9

1 Höre dir die Geschichte zweimal an und bearbeite dann die Aufgaben. ___ von 7

		right	wrong
a	A policeman met an old man on his way through town.	☐	☐
b	The man had a tiger on a leash *(Leine)*.	☐	☐
c	He had found the tiger in the park.	☐	☐
d	The tiger had hurt one of its front paws.	☐	☐
e	The policeman told the old man to take the tiger to the doctor.	☐	☐
f	The next day the policeman met the old man with the tiger again.	☐	☐
g	This time he wanted to watch TV with the tiger.	☐	☐

2 Lies den folgenden Text über Robin Hood und bearbeite dann die Aufgabe. ___ von 12

An invitation from the Queen

One morning when Robin Hood was riding in Sherwood Forest, he met a strange knight. Robin greeted him, but the knight got a fright and fell off his horse. Robin rode up to the knight. He lay unconscious *(bewusstlos)* on the ground. Robin jumped down from his horse at once and had a look at the knight's face:

"Marian!", he whispered when he saw that it was Marian, his girlfriend. "I didn't want to hurt you!" Robin took a cloth out of his pocket, ran to a little pond nearby and dipped it into the water. Then he came back and put it on Marian's forehead *(Stirn)*. After a while Marian opened her eyes and said:

"Is it really you, Robin?"

"Sure, my darling," Robin answered and gave her a kiss. "But what are you doing here in the forest?"

"I'm looking for you. I've come from the queen."

She gave Robin a letter. It was an invitation to the king's archery competition next Sunday. Robin read the letter and said: "Yes, of course. I'll come with some of my friends to compete with the king's archers. I'll show them that I'm the best!"

Streiche die falschen Satzteile aus und schreibe den Satz noch einmal richtig auf.

a One night Robin Hood met a strange knight.

____

b Marian jumped down from her horse.

____

c Marian put a wet cloth on Robin's forehead.

____

d Marian gave Robin a letter from the king.

____

e It was an invitation to the queen's picnic on Saturday.

____

f Robin will go there with Maid Marian.

____

3 Stelle die Fragen zu den Antworten oder beantworte die Fragen. ___ von 9

Example: *How old will you be next Sunday?* ⇨ I'll be thirteen next Sunday.

a What ____________________ ⇨ I think I'll get a CD.

b Where ____________________ ⇨ We'll travel to Italy this year.

____

c Will you go by plane? ⇨ No, ____________________.

⇨ We ____________________ by car.

d Will the weather be sunny tomorrow? ⇨ No, ____________________.

____________________ rainy.

e When ____________________ ⇨ Manchester United will play against Chelsea on Wednesday.

____

f Where ____________________ ⇨ They'll play in London.

g Who will win? ⇨ I think Manchester ____________________.

4 Sieh dir das Horoskop für nächsten Monat an. Schreibe in ganzen Sätzen auf, was es für Cedric, Karen, Benedict und Jane vorhersagt.

___ von 9

21 APRIL – 21 MAY

- be happy in love
- pocket money: not more
- marks in maths: OK

♉

Cedric:

He ______________________________

____

____

____

____

____

24 SEPTEMBER – 23 OCTOBER

- not go on holiday
- get present
- have new friend

♎

Karen:

She ______________________________

____

____

____

____

____

20 FEBRUARY – 20 MARCH

- make an excursion
- get a guitar
- not go to school

♓

Benedict and Jane:

They ______________________________

____

____

____

____

____

Notenschlüssel

1	2	3	4	5	6
37–34	33–29	28–24	23–19	18–9	8–0

So lange habe ich gebraucht: ______________

So viele Punkte habe ich erreicht: ______________

Test 7

- Kompetenzbereiche: Hörverstehen, Grammatik, Wortschatz, Schreiben
- Inhalte: Personalpronomen in der Objektform; Wortfelder ergänzen; eine E-Mail schreiben
- Zeitbedarf: 15 Minuten

Track 10

1 Höre dir an, was Alice, ein Mädchen aus Boston, über Halloween erzählt.
Lies dir die Sätze durch und streiche das Wort aus, das falsch ist. Höre dir den Text danach noch einmal an und schreibe den korrekten Satz auf. ___ von 4

a On Halloween children in the USA dress up as ~~clowns~~ and witches.

On Halloween children in the USA dress up as ghosts and witches.

b On 30th October they go from house to house.

____

c They shout "Trick or sweet!" and often get candies.

____

d This year an old woman didn't give them anything.

____

e So the children played a trick on him; they rang the phone several times and ran away.

____

2 Sarahs Familie ist letztes Jahr zusammen mit Freunden in deren Auto in Urlaub gefahren.
Wähle die richtigen Personalpronomen (persönliche Fürwörter) aus dem Kasten und setze sie in die Lücken ein. Drei Personalpronomen aus dem Kasten bleiben übrig. ___ von 7

me – our – us – his – him – her – she – it – their – them

a Last year we went on holiday with __________ friends in __________ car.

b On the way the car made a strange noise. So they had to take __________ to a garage at once.

c Our friends wanted to buy some souvenirs. So we went shopping with __________.

d Tim, their little son, likes building sandcastles. So they went to the beach with __________.

e My sister wanted a new dress, but my parents didn't buy one for __________.

f After a week we had to go home again. It was a nice holiday for all of __________.

3 Sieh dir die Wörterreihen an. Finde jeweils noch ein passendes Wort, das in die Reihe passt. ___ von 5

a aunt – mother – grandfather – daughter – cousin – ______________________

b flat – castle – tent – cottage – ______________________

c video recorder – digital camera – mobile phone – ______________________

d run – go – drive – ride – ______________________

e car – caravan – train – taxi – ______________________

4 Tom schreibt eine E-Mail an seinen besten Freund, um ihm zu erzählen, was ihm gestern passiert ist. Verwende *simple past*-Formen. Manchmal brauchst du auch Formen im *will-future*. ___ von 6

Er schreibt, dass
... er gestern zu spät aufgestanden ist.
... seine Mutter den Wecker nicht gehört hat.
... er zur Bushaltestelle gerannt ist.
... er den Bus verpasst *(missed)* hat.
... er morgen nicht wieder so spät aufstehen wird.
... er nächste Woche mit dem Fahrrad in die Schule fährt.

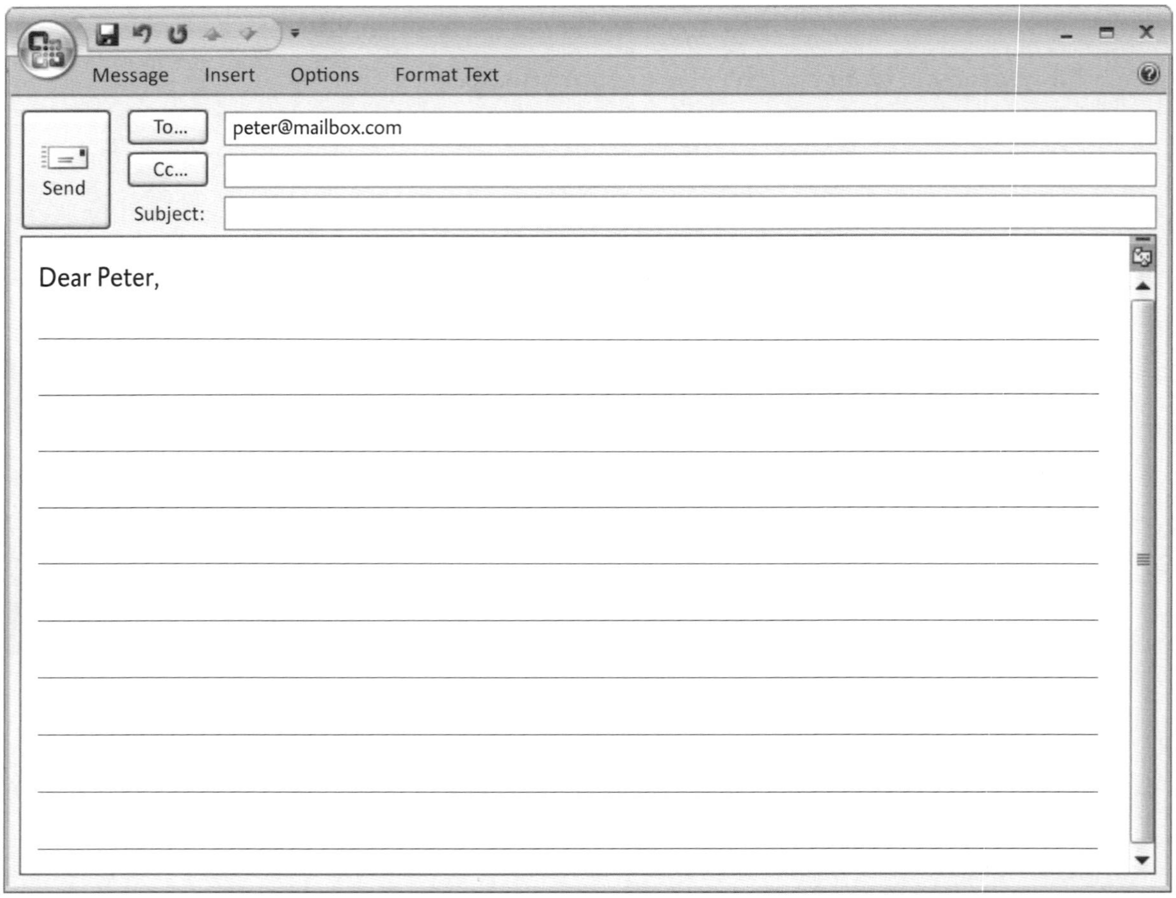

Notenschlüssel

1	2	3	4	5	6
22–20	19–17	16–14	13–11	10–5	4–0

So lange habe ich gebraucht: ______________

So viele Punkte habe ich erreicht: ______________

Klassenarbeit 7

- Kompetenzbereiche: Sprachmittlung, Wortschatz, Grammatik
- Inhalte: *simple past, simple present/present progressive, going to-future*; Kreuzworträtsel
- Zeitbedarf: 35 Minuten

1 Lies dir die Anzeige eines Ehepaars durch, das in den Ferien gerne seine Wohnung tauschen würde.

___ von 16

info

Hi! We are Jimmy and Frances Smith, both 46 years old. Our house is a modern home with three bedrooms (built in 2010). Downstairs is a kitchen with a door to a big back garden. There is also a living and a dining room and a toilet with a hand wash basin. Upstairs there is a big bedroom with a TV and two smaller bedrooms. There is also a bathroom with bath and shower. The garage is part of the house.

Our house is located in Montrose near the beach. In the town there is a cinema and there are pubs, restaurants, parks and shops. The nearest cities are Dundee and Aberdeen. They are only 45 km to the north or to the south. We are right in the middle. It's only a 45-minute drive. You can use our car, a red Renault, during your stay. But you can get there by train, too.

Reinhard erzählt seiner Tante Gitti, dass er und seine Familie einen Wohnungstausch in den Sommerferien mit einer schottischen Familie machen. Nachdem sich seine Tante auch für einen Wohnungstausch interessiert, fragt sie ihn genauer aus.

Beantworte Tante Gittis Fragen auf Deutsch. Antworte nicht nur mit einem Wort, sondern etwas ausführlicher.

Sie möchte wissen …

a … in welchem Ort sich das Haus befindet.

____

____

b … wie das Haus aussieht.

____

____

c … wie viele und welche Zimmer das Haus hat.

____

____

____

____

d ... ob es dort auch einen Fernseher gibt.

____

e ... was man dort unternehmen kann, wenn es regnet.

____

____

f ... welches die nächste größere Stadt ist.

____

____

g ... wie man dorthin kommt und wie weit es ist.

____

____

h ... ob sie ihr eigenes Auto mitnehmen sollen.

____

____

2 Vervollständige den Text mit den Wörtern aus dem Kasten. Sie sind jedoch in der Grundform. Schreibe jeweils die richtige *simple past*-Form in die Lücken. ___ von 9

take – want – ~~be~~ – see – go – find – say (2x) – think – look

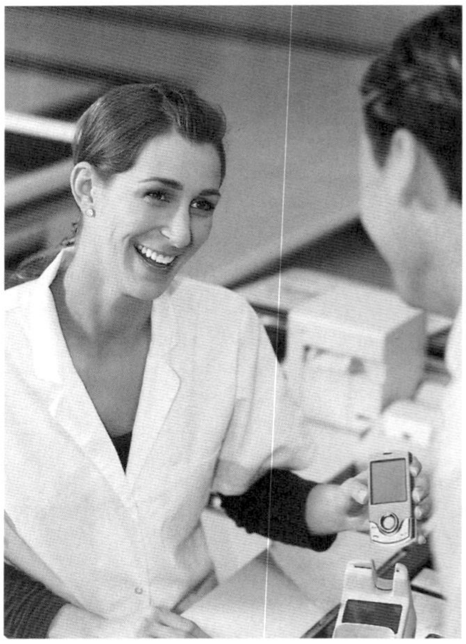

Mia _was_ at the supermarket last Monday. She ____________ to buy ice cream and ____________ for her favourite ice cream in the freezer. Suddenly she ____________ a mobile phone at the bottom of the freezer. "A mobile phone doesn't belong in a freezer", she ____________. "Somebody must have forgotten it". She ____________ the mobile phone and ____________ to the girl at the checkout *(Kasse)*: "I ____________ this mobile phone in the freezer. I think somebody left it there." The girl at the checkout ____________: "Oh dear! It's my mobile phone! I've missed it the whole day. I must have forgotten it there this morning. Thanks a lot." Then she ____________: "Go back to the freezer and take the biggest box of ice cream you want. I'll pay for it."

3 Vincents Großeltern haben einen Bauernhof und er besucht sie dort oft. Lies dir durch, was er erzählt, und setze die Verben entweder in das *simple present* oder das *present progressive.*

37
___ von 9

Vincent often goes (go) to see his grandparents in the country. They ___________ (have) a farm with a lot of animals. Vincent always ___________ (take) the train at 11.15 to Hereford when he ___________ (visit) his grandparents at the weekend. The train ___________ (arrive) in Hereford at 12.30. His grandmother always ___________ (wait) for him at the station. Then they ___________ (go) to the farm by car.

Vincent is showing you some photos from the farm:

"In the left picture you can see grandma. She is picking (pick) plums.
In the other picture you can see my cousin Tina. She ___________ (milk) a cow."

"This is me. ___________ (feed) the horse. In the other picture you can see my grandpa. He ___________ (carry) a lamb."

4 Fülle das Kreuzworträtsel mit den passenden Wörtern aus. ___ von 12

across *(waagrecht)*

2 a book where you can look up a word in English

7 your parents' son is your …

10 the opposite of "buy"

12 German and English are …

9

down *(senkrecht)*

1 time when there is no school

3 a hot drink

4 it's 365 or 366 days long

8 the opposite of "interesting"

11 the opposite of "short"

5

6

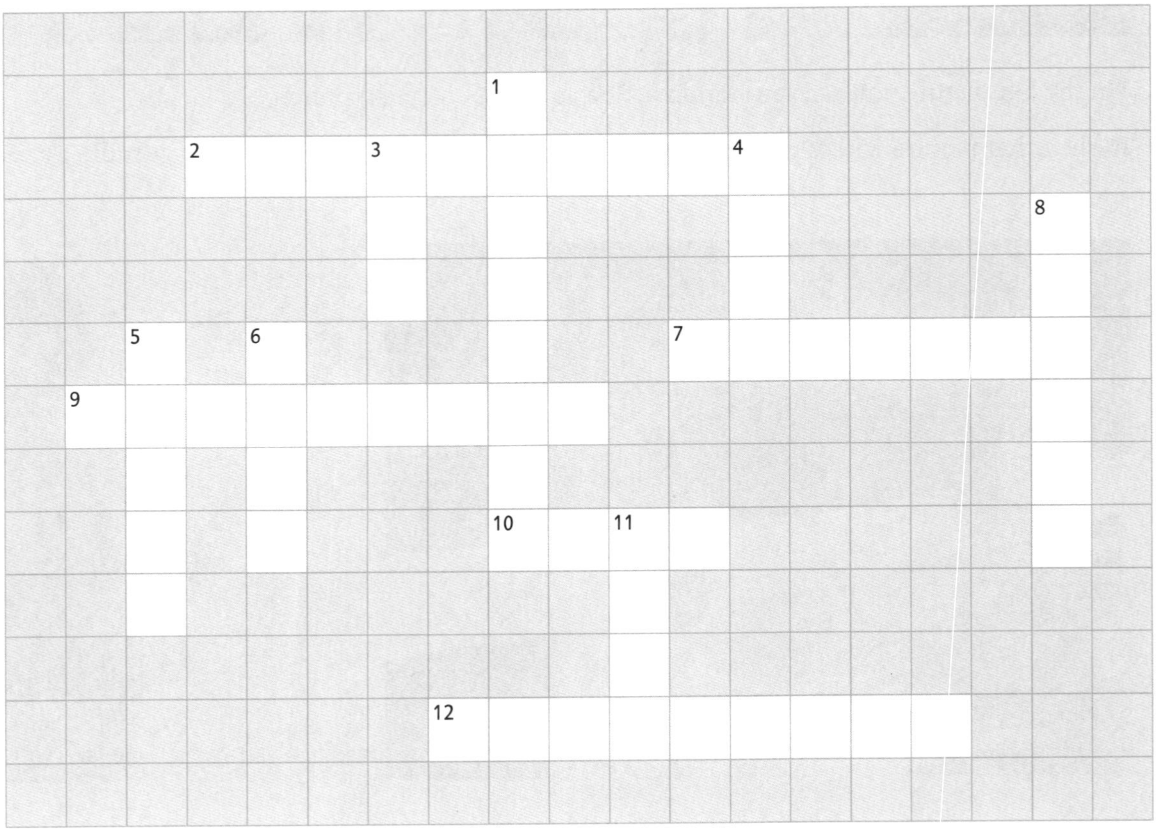

5 *What are they going to do tomorrow?*
Sieh dir die Notizen an, die sich die Kinder gemacht haben. Was haben sie morgen vor? Ergänze die Sätze.

___ von 5

a Holly *is going to see a film at the cinema.* ______________________________

____

b Michael *is going to* ______________________________

____

c Sarah and Susan *are going to* ______________________________

____

d Robby ______________________________

____

e Daniel and Brian ______________________________

____

f And what are <u>you</u> going to do tomorrow?

____

6 Doris und Brian reden über die Ferienpläne ihrer Familien. Schreibe auf Englisch auf, was sie sagen.

___ von

Doris …

… fragt Brian, was er letztes Wochenende gemacht hat.

Brian …

… sagt, dass er mit seiner Familie campen war.

Doris …

… fragt, wo sie campen waren.

Brian …

… sagt, dass sie am Loch Ness waren.

Doris …

… fragt, ob er Nessie gesehen hat.

Brian …

… sagt, dass er Nessie nicht gesehen hat.

Doris …

… fragt, was er nächstes Wochenende macht.

Brian …

… sagt, dass sie sich treffen könnten.

Doris …

… sagt, dass das toll wäre.

Notenschlüssel

1	2	3	4	5	6
61–54	53–46	45–38	37–30	29–14	13–0

So lange habe ich gebraucht: ___

So viele Punkte habe ich erreicht: ___